CW01163232

Original title:
Crystalline Calm

Copyright © 2024 Creative Arts Management OÜ
All rights reserved.

Author: Nora Sinclair

ISBN HARDBACK: 978-9916-90-594-4
ISBN PAPERBACK: 978-9916-90-595-1

Glistening Whispers

In twilight's glow, soft dreams abide,
A tender breeze, where secrets hide.
Leaves dance gently, shadows entwine,
Whispers of wishes, sweet and divine.

Stars awaken, a shimmering sea,
Each flicker tells tales, wild and free.
Moonlight glistens on waters wide,
Carrying hearts on a silvery tide.

Echoes of Stillness

Calm blankets the land, a hushed embrace,
Nature's heartbeat, a slow, tranquil pace.
Time stretches softly, where moments blend,
In silence, the whispers of echoes send.

Trees stand watch, their secrets profound,
In stillness, the wisdom of ages abound.
Breath of the earth, a timeless song,
In the quietude, we all belong.

Frosted Serenity

A blanket of white, the world lies still,
Each flake a reminder of winter's chill.
Footprints linger where laughter once played,
In frosted serenity, memories stayed.

Branches bowed low, kissed by the frost,
Nature's embrace, not a moment lost.
Crisp air carries whispers, soft and sweet,
In this frozen realm, hearts gently meet.

Radiance in Reflection

Sunset spills gold on the tranquil lake,
Moments of magic that memories make.
Ripples of light dance, spinning around,
In radiance's glow, pure beauty is found.

Mirrors of color in each glistening wave,
Nature's canvas, a masterpiece brave.
Life's fleeting moments, so vibrant, so rare,
In reflection, we find love everywhere.

Shards of Light in a Frozen World

In the stillness, light does play,
Icy fingers reach for day.
Shimmering under winter's gloom,
Hope emerges from the tomb.

Each breath freezes in the air,
A crystal dance, beyond compare.
Shards of brilliance, soft and bright,
Guide us through the winter's night.

Hushed Crystals of Twilight

In twilight's glow, the world slows down,
Wrapped in whispers, all around.
Crystals hang, reflecting lore,
Silent tales from days of yore.

A gentle hush, the stars awake,
While shadows stretch, and silence breaks.
Twilight whispers soft and sweet,
Nature’s heart, a rhythmic beat.

The Peace of a Frost-Kissed Dawn

Morning breaks with frosty breath,
A tranquil stillness, life from death.
Snowflakes waltz on gentle breeze,
Peaceful moments, hearts at ease.

Golden rays touch icy ground,
In this stillness, bliss is found.
Nature wakes, in quiet grace,
Frost-kissed dawn, a warm embrace.

Breaths of Ice in a Gentle Breeze

Whispers of ice in the cool air,
A dance of crystals, bright and rare.
Each breath a sparkle, each sigh a sigh,
In gentle breezes, dreams can fly.

Frosty fingers touch the trees,
While silence hums through winter's freeze.
Nature's voice, so soft and pure,
In icy breaths, we find our cure.

Moments of Clarity

In the hush of dawn's first light,
Thoughts drift like leaves in flight.
Eyes open wide, the world unfurls,
Every whisper stirs the pearls.

Time slows down, the heart takes note,
In simplicity, deep truths float.
Moments captured, brief yet bright,
Guiding souls through the night.

Fragile Fortitude

Beneath the weight of silent fears,
Strength blooms in tender tears.
Cracks in armor, a glimpse of grace,
Vulnerability finds its place.

Through storms endured, resilience grows,
A garden where the spirit glows.
Holding fast, yet learning to bend,
In fragility, we find our mend.

A Dance of Polished Light

In shadows cast by the fading sun,
Shimmering edges, where dreams run.
Each flicker tells a tale untold,
A dance of light, both warm and bold.

Waves of brilliance twirl and spin,
Illuminating the dark within.
A canvas painted with whispers bright,
Echoing softly through the night.

Serenity Bottled in Glass

Within the bottle, calm does dwell,
Captured moments, stories to tell.
Glimmers of peace in liquid form,
A refuge found amid the storm.

Shake it gently, let stillness rise,
Ripples weave through tranquil skies.
In every spark, a heartbeat flows,
Serenity in every glow.

The Peace Beneath the Surface

Beneath the waves, a calm prevails,
Hidden worlds tell silent tales.
Gentle currents weave and sway,
Life unfolds in soft ballet.

In shadows cast by sunlit streams,
Nature whispers tranquil dreams.
Bubbles rise in playful dance,
Echoes of a still romance.

A sanctuary free from strife,
In depths, there's beauty, rich with life.
An orchestra of muted sound,
Where solace and serenity abound.

Glacial Reverie

In fields of white, the stillness reigns,
Silent guardians of ancient chains.
Frozen spires pierce the sky,
Whispers of the world gone by.

Footprints trace a journey rare,
Through crystal halls, the frosty air.
A slumber deep in quiet grace,
Time stands still in this vast space.

Glacial rivers flow with ease,
Carving tales in icy breeze.
Each flake a dream, so pure, so bright,
Reflecting softly, the fading light.

Veil of Tranquil Reflections

Across the lake, a mirror gleams,
Framed by trees and sunlit beams.
Stillness wraps the evening air,
A gentle pause, a moment rare.

Rippling echoes, whispers low,
Nature’s secrets softly flow.
Clouds drift slow, a tender sigh,
As twilight paints the evening sky.

Within this peace, the heart can mend,
A soothing balm, the soul's best friend.
In reflections, truth finds space,
A haven of such warm embrace.

Frozen Whispers of Serenity

In hushed tones, the snowflakes fall,
A blanket soft, a muted call.
Each crystal glimmers, pure and bright,
Whispers of a silent night.

The world is wrapped in frozen peace,
Where worries fade and troubles cease.
Footsteps crunch in soft repose,
Nature’s breath, a sweet expose.

Time drifts gently, like the snow,
In winter's arms, the heart can glow.
Here in stillness, beauty reigns,
Frozen whispers soothe our pains.

Frozen Hues of Harmony

In the glimmering frost the colors collide,
Shades of blue and white, where silence resides.
Each flake that falls carries whispers of joy,
A canvas of winter, nature's own ploy.

Branches adorned in a crystal embrace,
A tranquil tableau, a peaceful space.
Harmony sings in the still of the night,
While stars twinkle softly, a shimmering light.

The Stillness of Crystals

In a quiet room, the crystals reflect,
Echoes of calm, a gentle effect.
Each facet holds secrets of time and grace,
Stillness envelops, a sacred place.

Light dances softly on surfaces clear,
Whispers of wisdom, for all who draw near.
A symphony silent, yet vividly bright,
Crystals hold beauty in the hush of night.

Luminescent Dreams

In the depths of slumber, soft beams ignite,
Colors of wonder, a magical sight.
Dreams blend with starlight, weaving the night,
Embraced by the moon, in a world full of light.

Each thought like a feather, floats serenely,
Painting the dark with a shimmer so keenly.
In luminescent visions, hearts take flight,
Awakening softly to morning's first light.

Purest Reflections

Ripples of water, a mirror so clear,
Unraveling stories, as memories peer.
Nature's own canvas, painted with grace,
The purest reflections of time and space.

Beneath the surface, the world lies concealed,
Echoes of choices, the heart is revealed.
In whispers of current, the truth flows bright,
Guiding us gently toward love and light.

Glistening Memories in the Cold

Frosted whispers in the air,
Footprints lost, a fleeting care.
Icicles hang from eaves above,
Shimmering tales of winter's love.

Snowflakes dance on softest breeze,
Blanketing the world with ease.
Memories, like the icy dew,
Glisten bright with every view.

The Serenity Found in Glacial Light

Crystalline shadows paint the ground,
A stillness in the night profound.
Moonlit glows on icy streams,
Whisper secrets in quiet dreams.

Stillness wraps the world so tight,
Bathed in calm, a gentle light.
Nature's hush, a soothing balm,
In the cold, a tranquil calm.

Echoes of Silence in Crystal Dreams

In the hush of winter's breath,
Silent echoes dance with death.
Dreams like snowflakes touch the ground,
In crystal realms, peace is found.

Through the glades, the shadows creep,
Guarding secrets that we keep.
Whispers soft, as night descends,
In stillness, the heart transcends.

The Lull of Winter's Touch

Winter's fingers gently trace,
Every branch, each frozen face.
Softly, softly, nature sleeps,
As the world in silence weeps.

Breath of frost, a lulling sigh,
Underneath the starry sky.
In the quiet, dreams take flight,
Wrapped in winter’s pure delight.

The Lullaby of Shattered Icicles

Softly they fall, the shards of ice,
Whispers of winter, a chilling slice.
Crystals collide in a quiet hum,
Singing the secrets of frost's cold drum.

Beneath the boughs, the snow does rest,
Nature's blanket, a soft, white vest.
Each breath of air, a frosty sigh,
As nights grow longer, and shadows lie.

Echoes of a Frosted Reverie

In the hush of dawn, frost paints the ground,
Echoes of dreams where silence is found.
Glimmers of ice dance in the light,
Whispers of magic in the cold night.

Memories linger where the cold winds blow,
Tracing the steps of the fallen snow.
Time drifts gently, a fleeting tide,
Where echoes of winter in stillness bide.

Subtle Glares of Winter’s Veil

A veil of white, so pure and bright,
Subtle glares in the morning light.
Frost-kissed branches, a jeweled lace,
Nature’s art, a graceful space.

Through frozen paths, shadows creep,
While the world, in stillness, seems to sleep.
A quiet beauty, both stark and clear,
Whispers of warmth soon drawing near.

Beneath the Glimmering Surface

Beneath the ice, the world hides still,
Secrets of life wrapped in winter's chill.
A delicate dance of frozen grace,
Waiting for spring's tender embrace.

Reflections shimmer in the cool pond,
Mirrors of dreams, of memories fond.
With each soft ripple, a story unfolds,
Beneath the glimmering, wintery holds.

Muffled Steps on Powdered Snow

Footprints linger, soft and light,
Whispers woven through the night.
Silent shadows dance and sway,
In the heart of winter's play.

Each step taken, hushed and slow,
Breath of frost, a gentle blow.
Branches bare, with stillness crowned,
Nature's peace, a soothing sound.

The Calm Within a Frozen Echo

In the stillness, time stands still,
Echoes drift, a softened thrill.
Frozen whispers serenade the air,
A tranquil moment, calm and rare.

Within the hush, a heartbeat flows,
Tales of winter, deep in prose.
Nature's lullaby, soft and slow,
Wraps the world in peaceful glow.

Glacial Dreams Unfurled

Dreams of ice, a crystal sea,
Wonders wrapped in frosty glee.
Slumbering echoes, bright and bold,
Stories of the cold retold.

Glacial visions drift and sway,
Painted skies in hues of gray.
In the silence, visions gleam,
Carved in time, a winter's dream.

Ethereal Light on Soft Snowfall

Whispers of light, a gentle glow,
Dancing softly on the snow.
Crystal flakes in twilight's hand,
Each a dream from winter's land.

Ethereal hues embrace the night,
Painting stillness with delight.
Nature's canvas, pure and bright,
Shimmers gently in the light.

Still Waters

In quiet depths, reflections glow,
The world above moves fast, yet slow.
Gentle ripples dance and sway,
Holding secrets of the day.

Beneath the surface, life abides,
In whispered currents, truth resides.
A moment's peace, a tranquil heart,
Still waters hold their mystic art.

Starry Skies

Above the night, a canvas wide,
Where twinkling dreams and wishes bide.
Each star a tale, a distant light,
Guiding souls through endless night.

Constellations weave their story,
In silence bright, they claim their glory.
A gaze aloft, hearts take flight,
Beneath the vast, embracing night.

Nature’s Glassy Embrace

In morning's mist, the earth awakes,
A tender sigh, the stillness breaks.
Leaves aglow in sun's warm kiss,
Nature holds her moment of bliss.

Rivers mirror the towering trees,
Whispers carried on the breeze.
In every shadow, light remains,
Nature's glassy embrace sustains.

Twilight in Shards

The day’s sweet light begins to fade,
In hues of gold, the dusk is laid.
Shattered colors paint the skies,
As night unfolds with silent sighs.

In twilight's grip, the world feels near,
A gentle hush, the darkness clears.
Echoes linger, soft and bold,
In twilight’s shards, new tales unfold.

Distant Echoes

Faint whispers float on evening's breeze,
Carried far beyond the trees.
Like memories held in a gentle song,
Distant echoes where hearts belong.

Through valleys deep and mountains high,
The past and present softly sigh.
In every note, a story breathes,
Distant echoes weave and seethe.

Soft Visions

In dreams that drift like clouds above,
We chase the light, the warmth of love.
Soft visions linger, shadows blend,
A fleeting world that does not end.

With every blink, a picture fades,
Yet hope remains in twilight shades.
In slumber's hold, we find our way,
To soft visions where we can stay.

A Still Lake of Dreams

The surface shines like glass at night,
Soft whispers linger, taking flight.
Reflections dance in moonlit grace,
While stars keep watch in their quiet space.

Stillness reigns where ripples fade,
A sanctuary, a tranquil glade.
Each breath a sigh, each thought a wish,
Embracing dreams with every swish.

Fractured Light on Polished Waters

Sunlight fractures, colors play,
On waters still, where shadows sway.
Rippling echoes of days gone by,
Painting stories beneath the sky.

Each glimmer holds a secret tight,
In fractured beams, a fleeting sight.
The dance of light, a timeless show,
A tapestry where memories flow.

Radiance of a Winter's Heart

Snowflakes fall with gentle grace,
Whispered tales in a frozen space.
The world transforms, a blanket wide,
In winter's arms, we softly hide.

Warmth resides in hearts alive,
Amidst the chill, the spirits thrive.
A radiant glow in the coldest hour,
Love's warmth blooms like a winter flower.

Soft Radiance in a Frosted World

Frosted trees in morning light,
Each crystal spark, a pure delight.
Nature's breath, a gilded scene,
Where silence reigns, and all is clean.

A soft glow breaks the dawn's embrace,
As shadows dance with gentle pace.
Embracing hope in winter's hold,
A story waits, yet to be told.

Chiming Crystals in the Breeze

Softly they dance, the crystals bright,
Glistening stars in the morning light.
With laughter they twirl, so free and glad,
Echoing joy that we all once had.

Gentle whispers, the wind's sweet song,
Carry their secrets where they belong.
A symphony formed in nature's caress,
Chiming crystals, our hearts they impress.

In the meadow, a magical sight,
Each shimmer reflecting pure delight.
Together they sway, they shimmer and glow,
In the embrace of a soft, gentle flow.

Nature adorned in her finest threads,
A tapestry woven where beauty spreads.
Chiming crystals, they sing of peace,
In their harmony, our worries cease.

A Tapestry of Frosty Peace

In stillness wraps the wintry air,
A tapestry woven with gentle care.
White blankets cover the sleeping ground,
In frosty silence, serenity found.

Icicles hang like jewels divine,
Nature pauses, as if to dine.
A canvas painted in hues of white,
In frosty peace, the world feels right.

Footprints trace through the snowy maze,
Each step whispers of winter's praise.
In every flake, a story to tell,
A tapestry echoes a crystal bell.

As twilight deepens, shadows blend,
The frosty peace will never end.
Wrapped in wonder, the world takes heed,
In the silence, our hearts are freed.

Luminous Hush of Twilight’s Kiss

A hush falls gently on the land,
Twilight envelops, like a soft hand.
Stars awaken, shyly they gleam,
In luminous hues, we drift and dream.

The sky blushes in shades of gold,
Whispers of secrets, tenderly told.
Night's embrace cradles the day,
In twilight’s kiss, worries drift away.

Shadows lengthen, the moon takes flight,
Casting its glow, a silvery light.
While crickets sing soft lullabies,
In this moment, time gently flies.

Wrapped in warmth, the world feels near,
In twilight’s hush, we shed our fear.
Luminous wonders, forever they last,
In the arms of night, we’re free at last.

The Serenity of Icy Landscapes

Icy terrains stretch far and wide,
In serenity's grasp, where dreams abide.
Glacial rivers sing their lullaby,
Reflecting beauty as they flow by.

Mountains wear crowns of glistening white,
Nature whispers in the soft twilight.
Each frozen branch, a work of art,
In icy landscapes, peace fills the heart.

The world is hushed, a tranquil scene,
Where time stands still, and souls convene.
A canvas of ice, both fierce and grand,
In the serenity of this frozen land.

Every breeze carries a gentle sigh,
Underneath the vast, expansive sky.
In icy landscapes, our spirits soar,
Finding solace forevermore.

Shimmering Clouds of Winter’s Breath

The clouds whisper soft, a gentle sigh,
Painting the sky with dreams that fly.
In silver threads, the light does weave,
A tapestry spun, where hearts believe.

Each flake a dancer, twirling down,
Adorning the earth, a snowy crown.
Under the glow of a pale moon’s grace,
Winter’s breath holds a tender embrace.

Soft Radiance in the Frozen Dark

In shadows deep, a flicker glows,
A candle's warmth amidst the snows.
Each flicker whispers tales untold,
Of dreams and hopes in the icy cold.

Veils of darkness softly part,
Revealing light that stirs the heart.
In frozen realms, love finds its spark,
A soft radiance in the frozen dark.

A Moment Encased in Solitude

In quiet spaces, time stands still,
Wrapping the soul with a tender chill.
The world outside begins to fade,
In solitude’s arms, dreams are laid.

A breath of peace, a sacred pause,
In silent whispers, reflecting cause.
A moment captured, pure and bright,
Encased in solitude’s soft light.

Still Waters of a Frosted Dream

The lake lies still, a crystal sheet,
Reflecting stars, a silent beat.
In frosted dreams, the night does gleam,
A tranquil world, where moments teem.

With every shimmer, secrets flow,
Beneath the surface, time moves slow.
In this calm, all sorrows seem,
To drift away on a frosted dream.

Glistening Echoes of Stillness

In the quiet woods we tread,
Whispers weave through branches bare.
Footsteps soft, the thoughts spread,
Nature's melody fills the air.

Beneath the canopy so wide,
Every rustle tells a tale.
Here in peace, we need not hide,
Calm and stillness softly prevail.

Reflections dance on waters clear,
Mirrors of a world serene.
Lost in thoughts, we linger near,
Captured in this tranquil scene.

Time stands still in nature's fold,
Golden sun begins to rise.
Echoes of the day unfold,
In this haven, wonder lies.

Shimmering Silence Beneath Frost

Winter's veil of sparkling white,
Hides the secrets of the ground.
Stars above, the softest light,
Crystals form without a sound.

Every step, a gentle crunch,
Air so crisp, it takes your breath.
Nature sways in quiet brunch,
Life seems frozen among death.

Branches laden, heavy, still,
Holding dreams of spring's embrace.
Time, it moves with gentle will,
In this frozen, sacred space.

Beneath the frost, the earth awaits,
Life’s renewal on the brink.
In the stillness, hope creates,
A melody too sweet to think.

The Icy Breath of Dawn

Morning whispers, clear and bright,
Crystals shine in rosy hues.
Dewdrops glisten with pure light,
Nature wakes with fresh renewed views.

Breath of cool, the day begins,
Frosty air a gentle kiss.
Awakening the world within,
Moments here, we cannot miss.

Softly glows the waking sun,
Painting skies with amber brush.
In the silence, senses run,
Feel the heartbeat, feel the hush.

Every note in morning song,
Echoes through the tranquil morn.
In this moment, right and wrong,
Fade away, a new day born.

Harmony Encased in Glass

In a world of fragile grace,
Where reflections intertwine.
Beauty held in time and space,
Captured moments, pure divine.

Shimmering light through surfaces,
Every angle tells a twist.
Layers hide our stories' traces,
In their depths, what we've missed.

Whispers echo, soft and clear,
Memories dance in the light.
Each sharp edge a tale we hear,
Fragments woven, day and night.

Harmony beneath the sheen,
Glass encased, our hearts displayed.
In this art, we're never keen,
To hide the love that we've made.

Traces of Calm in the Icebound Night

Beneath the stars, a whisper flows,
Through frozen trees, where silence grows.
Each flake of snow, a gentle sigh,
In winter's hold, the world sleeps nigh.

The moonbeams dance on icy streams,
Casting soft light on hidden dreams.
A tranquil air, where shadows dwell,
In night's embrace, all hearts compel.

Cold winds murmur through the pines,
Secrets held in nature's lines.
A breath of peace, the world at rest,
In icebound nights, the soul is blessed.

Traces linger, a fleeting hope,
As stars align and spirits cope.
In frosty calm, the heart takes flight,
Finding solace in the night.

Winter's Caress on Silent Waters

Gentle waves, a mirrored sheen,
Reflecting dreams where few have been.
Winter's hand, soft as a sigh,
Holds the waters, where whispers lie.

With every gust, the ripples play,
In silent depths, they drift away.
A frosted breath upon the lake,
In stillness, all the world will wake.

Snowflakes dance upon the tide,
Nature's art, a graceful guide.
Winter's caress, a fleeting touch,
Brings peace to hearts that long for much.

On icy shores, we find our way,
As twilight falls at end of day.
In tranquility, our spirits soar,
Silent waters, forevermore.

The Shimmer of Stillness at Dusk

As daylight fades, the sky ignites,
With hues of gold, the heart delights.
The world in pause, a sacred space,
While shadows stretch, they softly trace.

Beneath the trees, the silence reigns,
As dusk envelops, soothing pains.
A shimmer bright in twilight's embrace,
Casts gentle warmth upon our face.

Each fleeting moment, a breath held tight,
In stillness found, we meet the night.
With every star that starts to gleam,
We find ourselves in twilight's dream.

In quietude, our spirits dance,
In dusky light, we take a chance.
Amidst the calm, the world feels right,
Embraced by the shimmer of soft night.

Silent Shadows in Frosted Light

In frosted dawn, the shadows creep,
Through tranquil woods, the world doth sleep.
Each breath of air, a crisp delight,
As whispers roam in morning light.

Silent paths where footsteps fade,
In winter's grip, beauty conveyed.
The sun rises, a golden hue,
Awakening spirits, fresh as dew.

With every breeze, the branches sway,
Dancing softly in the day.
Shadows stretch in tender grace,
A fleeting moment, time's embrace.

In stillness found, we pause to see,
The magic spun in nature's glee.
Frosted light, a canvas bright,
Paints silent shadows in our sight.

Veils of Icy Tranquility

In the hush of winter's breath,
Whispers of frost ascend the night.
Silent stars in stillness rest,
Underneath the pale moonlight.

Shadows dance on fields of white,
A shimmering cloak surrounds the trees.
Each crystal flake, a fleeting sight,
A moment caught in memories.

Frozen streams like glass do flow,
Reflecting dreams in twilight's gleam.
Nature's pause, a gentle show,
In icy veils, the world will dream.

Beneath this calm, the heart does soar,
Finding peace in nature's grace.
Veils of tranquility restore,
In the wild, we find our place.

Calm Within the Gem

Deep within a crystal clear,
Lies a world of quiet light.
Reflections shimmer, drawing near,
Caught in patterns, pure and bright.

Each facet holds a story told,
Echoes of a tranquil tune.
Secrets of the heart unfold,
Beneath the watchful gaze of moon.

A tranquil pulse, the gem does hold,
Whispers soft as evening's sigh.
In its depths, a calm so bold,
Cradling hopes that yearn to fly.

Time stands still in this embrace,
Moments linger, gently blend.
Finding peace in this safe space,
The calm within, our perfect end.

Ethereal Chiaroscuro

Light and shadow intertwine,
Painted whispers on the ground.
In the dusk, the edges shine,
Bringing life to what is found.

Ghostly figures dance in mist,
Shapes emerge from twilight's glow.
In the silence, dreams persist,
As night weaves a gentle flow.

Each brushstroke tells a tale anew,
Of existence, strife, and peace.
In chiaroscuro's deep hue,
We find our fears and sweet release.

Embrace the light and dark we face,
In this balance, truth expands.
Ethereal moments we embrace,
With open hearts and willing hands.

Breath of the Aurora

In the night, a whisper glows,
Colors dance across the sky.
Winds of change begin to flow,
As the stars begin to sigh.

Veils of green and shades of gold,
Blend like dreams in twilight's grace.
Nature's wonders, tales untold,
Lift our spirits, find our place.

Each flicker, life’s sweet embrace,
An enchanting, fleeting glance.
In the cosmos, we find space,
To join in this celestial dance.

Breath of the aurora calls,
Stirring hearts beneath the night.
In its light, our wonder sprawls,
Guiding souls with pure delight.

Whispered Promises in Pearls of Ice

In the silence, secrets dwell,
Softly wrapped in icy shell.
Promises etched in frozen breath,
Whispers linger, defying death.

Mirrored visions in frost's embrace,
Time stands still in this sacred place.
Each glimmer tells a story old,
In shimmering pearls, dreams unfold.

Chilled sentiments drift like snow,
Carried softly, where memories flow.
Underneath a blanket of white,
Heartbeats echo in the night.

Among the echoes, a warmth ignites,
Held close, beneath the starry lights.
Together in this quiet trance,
Forever caught in frozen dance.

Silent Symphony of Glimmering Light

In quietude, the stars appear,
Composing melodies crystal clear.
A symphony of shadows play,
Through the night, they sway and sway.

Every flicker, a note to sing,
In the darkness, the universe swings.
Glimmers whisper, secrets untold,
In the silence, wonders unfold.

Dancing rays in a cosmic flight,
Each shining moment, a spark of light.
Together they weave a song divine,
A tapestry where dreams align.

Beneath the vast, unending skies,
Every gaze invites the wise.
In the stillness, hear the song,
Where every soul, on stars, belongs.

The Stillness of Falling Snowflakes

Softly dancing through the air,
Whispers of winter everywhere.
Each flake unique, a fleeting grace,
In the stillness, they find their place.

Blanketing earth in a gentle shroud,
Silence wraps the world like a crowd.
Time slows down with every fall,
Nature breathes, answering all.

Frozen moments embrace the night,
Crystals glimmer in soft moonlight.
In this hush, worries fade away,
Peace descends, where shadows play.

Falling dreams in a snowy swirl,
Each crystal a wish, a delicate pearl.
The stillness sings a lullaby sweet,
In winter's grasp, our hearts meet.

Embrace of the Chilled Morning

With dawn’s light, frost begins to gleam,
A tranquil world, like a perfect dream.
Chilled whispers cross the waking earth,
In the cool, we find rebirth.

Breath like clouds in the crisp of day,
Nature stretches, shaking night away.
Birdsongs weave through the icy air,
A symphony beyond compare.

Each ray carries warmth, golden bright,
Chasing shadows, inviting light.
In the quiet, a promise dawns,
As the heart sings in hopeful yawns.

Dewdrops glisten on fragile blades,
Reflecting colors that never fade.
In this embrace of morning's grace,
We find solace in nature's face.

Solitude Wrapped in Frost

In the hush of winter's morn,
Silvery mist adorns the dawn.
Footprints fade in frosty white,
Whispers echo, soft and slight.

Barren branches gently sway,
Under clouds that drift and play.
Nature's breath, a crystal sigh,
Cradled beneath a muted sky.

Time slows down in quiet realms,
Where solitude cross the helms.
Lost in thoughts, a world so vast,
Wrapped in silence, shadows cast.

In this stillness, find the grace,
Of peaceful moments, slow embrace.
Winter's chill, a tender friend,
In solitude, all fears may mend.

Enchanted Silence in Still Air

Stars twinkle in a velvet night,
Each flicker a soft, guiding light.
A blanket of silence unfolds,
Enchanting tales gently told.

Snowflakes weave their dance with glee,
In a world where one feels free.
Breath held close, a moment grand,
Time suspended, vast and planned.

Whispers flutter in the night,
Carried on winds, soft and light.
Magic lingers in the air,
Leaving footprints, bold and rare.

Under moon's watch, spirits glide,
Wrapped in truth that won't subside.
In this silence, hearts align,
An enchanted space, purely divine.

The Lattice of Frozen Thoughts

In shadows deep, reflections grow,
Frosty patterns dance below.
Thoughts like crystals, sharp and bright,
Frameless visions in the night.

Each layer holds a hidden truth,
Woven tales of ancient youth.
Frozen echoes linger long,
In the lattice, heartbeats strong.

Words unsaid drift through the air,
Like the chill, they intertwine with care.
Whispers caught in icy breath,
Life’s complexities in death.

Plunge into this frosty maze,
Where reflective thoughts amaze.
In the silence, find the key,
To unlock frozen reverie.

Mirrors of Winter’s Embrace

Glistening fields of crystal light,
Mirrors twinkle in the night.
Nature dons her frosty gown,
Blanketing both field and town.

Every flake a gem, unique,
Whispers soft in moon's mystique.
Branches bend beneath the weight,
Of winter's love, delicate fate.

In the stillness, hearts find peace,
As time slows, troubles cease.
Within these mirrors, truths reflect,
A world of wonder to connect.

Through winter’s realm, we gently tread,
With open hearts, both fierce and dread.
In every glance, find joy and grace,
In mirrors of this season's embrace.

Illusions in a Shimmering Freeze

Reflections dance on icy glass,
Fractured dreams in silver light.
In the silence, shadows pass,
Lost whispers swirl into the night.

Caught between the dusk and dawn,
Mirrored truths that fade away.
A phantom glimpse, a riddle drawn,
Where night is forged into the day.

Colors blur, the world stands still,
Time hangs heavy in the round.
In this chill, there’s a strange thrill,
As warmth gives way to frosty sound.

Dancing with the fleeting gleams,
A tapestry of dreams unfurled.
Illusions roll like whispered streams,
Embraced in this enchanted world.

Whispering Frost Beneath the Stars

Underneath the starlit veil,
Frosty murmurs kiss the pines.
In the quiet, soft chills sail,
Carrying secrets through the lines.

Each breath forms a crystal mist,
Wishes dance on icy air.
Frozen dreams we can't resist,
Ethereal hopes, everywhere.

Nighttime cradles whispered tales,
Carried whispers on the breeze.
As the moonlight softly pales,
Nature's song brings hearts to ease.

Stars are scattered, sparks that gleam,
In this frozen, tranquil place.
Every moment feels a dream,
Whispering frost, a warm embrace.

A Glimmering Haven of Peace

In the stillness, soft and bright,
Cascading layers, gentle glow.
Each flake catches the silver light,
Crafting moments, soft and slow.

A haven formed in winter's breath,
Where shadows yield to warmth and grace.
Here, the heart finds rest from death,
In tranquil spaces, time finds pace.

Crisp air cushions hope's sweet sighs,
Trees adorned with diamonds gleam.
Beneath the vast and endless skies,
Peace envelops like a dream.

Nature whispers gentle tunes,
A melody wrapped in the cold.
In the glow of silvered moons,
Peace thrives within, a sight to behold.

The Still Heart of a Frozen World

Silent echoes fill the air,
Where the frozen rivers flow.
Nature holds a breath of prayer,
As the softest blankets grow.

Winter's touch, a gentle hand,
Pausing time, a quiet muse.
In this hushed and wondrous land,
Secrets wrapped in frosty hues.

Branches bow beneath the weight,
Crystalline stars adorn the dark.
In the stillness, love's first date,
Finds its way to leave a mark.

Heartbeats pause in the icy thrall,
Where peace becomes the silent song.
Within this world, we all stand tall,
The heart remains where we belong.

Radiant Peace Amongst the Snow

Softly falls the snow tonight,
Blanketing the world in white.
Whispers carried through the trees,
A breath of calm, a gentle breeze.

Under moon's soft, silver light,
Hearts find solace in the night.
Footprints deep, yet fleeting fast,
In this peace, the die is cast.

Branches bow with heavy grace,
Nature holds a still embrace.
In the quiet, joy can grow,
In radiant peace among the snow.

Each flake a promise from above,
Dancing softly, purest love.
In the hush, time seems to pause,
In the stillness, find your cause.

Mirror of the Serene Winter

Glistening beneath the gray,
Fields of frost in bold array.
Nature dons her crystal crown,
In the hush, no trace of frown.

Stillness rests upon the lake,
Reflects the calm in every flake.
Mountains whisper tales of old,
Secrets shared in silence told.

Branches weave a lace so fine,
Echoing the warmth divine.
The world's a mirror, pure and bright,
In winter's grasp, we find delight.

Soft as shadows, dreams take flight,
In this realm of endless night.
Serene whispers in the air,
Hold the magic everywhere.

The Hushed Glow of Distant Lights

Stars above in velvet skies,
Sparkle softly, calming sighs.
In the dark, they seem to bloom,
Filling hearts with hopeful gloom.

Lanterns flicker far away,
Guiding lost souls on their way.
Whispers travel on the breeze,
Carried gently through the trees.

In the night, a tale unfolds,
Of love once whispered, love retold.
The glow of dreams, a beacon bright,
In the hush of silent night.

Through the dark, we learn to see,
The beauty in our mystery.
Hushed reflections all around,
In the quiet, hearts are found.

Crystal Fragments of Quietude

Icicles dangle, sharp yet clear,
Fractals glisten, drawing near.
Every breath is crystal fine,
Moments held in concentrated time.

Snowflakes weave a tapestry,
Whispers of a soft decree.
In the stillness, shadows play,
Drawing dreams that softly sway.

Each fragment tells a story bright,
Of a world wrapped up in light.
In quietude, our spirits soar,
Finding peace forevermore.

Embrace the silence, tender, pure,
In this calm, our hearts endure.
Crystal dreams shall guide our way,
In the quiet, we'll forever stay.

Silence Encased in Ice

Whispers of frost on glassy panes,
Shimmering cold that softly reigns.
Echoes linger in the still,
Time suspended, nature's thrill.

Footsteps muffled, shadows glide,
In the stillness, secrets hide.
A breath of chill, a fleeting sigh,
In silence deep, the world stands by.

Glistening crystals, a tranquil dance,
Nature's beauty in a frozen trance.
The world at rest, as if to dream,
In icy silence, life may seem.

Fragments of peace in the icy air,
Moments captured, beyond compare.
In this stillness, hearts find grace,
Silence encased in a crystal embrace.

Tranquil Prisms

Light refracts through a crystal sphere,
Colors bloom, yet whispers near.
Beneath the rain, a canvas bright,
Reflections shimmering in soft light.

Gentle hues in morning's glow,
Painting visions that ebb and flow.
A silent dance, so sweet and pure,
In every moment, we find allure.

Fragments of calm in a vivid play,
Nature's palette, brightening day.
Through prisms clear, dreams softly land,
Inviting hearts to understand.

In tranquil shades, our spirits rise,
Bathed in light, we touch the skies.
Echoes linger, serenity's hymn,
In tranquil prisms, life feels brimmed.

Shimmers of Peace

Softly glows the evening star,
Guiding souls from near and far.
In gentle tides, the waves retreat,
Painting shores with whispers sweet.

The sky deepens, colors blend,
In horizons vast, we find no end.
Moments hover, time stands still,
Within our hearts, a tranquil will.

Through rustling leaves, a melody sings,
In nature's arms, peace softly clings.
As daylight fades, shadows embrace,
In shimmers of peace, we find our place.

Each breath a gift, a soft release,
In unity, we share this peace.
Let go the noise, embrace the light,
In shimmers of peace, we unite.

The Art of Gentle Light

Brush strokes of dawn paint the sky,
With whispers soft, the night waves bye.
A gentle glow that warms the soul,
In stillness found, we become whole.

Fingers of light through branches reach,
Offering lessons that nature teach.
In every flicker, a promise bright,
The art of gentle, tender light.

Ripples of gold on a quiet stream,
Bathe our hearts in a golden dream.
Moments linger, in beauty wrapped,
In gracefulness, we feel entrapped.

With every dusk, a canvas new,
Colors spill, a gentle hue.
Artistry found in every sight,
In life's embrace, the gentle light.

Glistening Solitude of Winter Nights

In a blanket of white, the world holds its breath,
Whispers of silence in the chill of the depth.
Stars twinkle softly, like dreams in a flight,
Embracing the stillness of winter's soft night.

Frosted trees shimmer under the moon's watchful gaze,
Each branch a crystal, caught in a daze.
Crickets have silenced, the night feels so free,
Wrapped in the magic, just nature and me.

Footprints in snow tell a story untold,
Of wanderers brave, with hearts bold and cold.
The air is so crisp, each breath a small song,
In glistening solitude, I finally belong.

With each step I take, the crunching sounds weave,
A tapestry of winter that makes one believe.
Through the shimmering dark, I wander with ease,
Lost in the beauty of frost-kissed trees.

The Quiet Dance of Shimmering Cold

Underneath the dim glow of a silver-lit sky,
Ice crystals gather, as breezes float by.
Gently they twirl in a delicate waltz,
The quiet of winter, in every soft pulse.

Moonbeams reflect on a river of glass,
Time seems to pause, as moments do pass.
A world wrapped in wonder, still and serene,
In the quiet dance, it feels like a dream.

The night wears a coat of the finest white lace,
Each flake a performer in nature's own space.
With each breath I take, the cold stings my nose,
But the beauty surrounding me only grows.

I stand in this realm where the shadows blend,
The whispers of nighttime begin to transcend.
In the quiet dance, I hear nature's song,
A melody woven where I feel I belong.

Traces of Frost in a Moonlit Glow

When the world is adorned with a diamond-like sheen,
Every surface reflects in a magical scene.
Ghostly outlines where shadows once played,
Traces of frost in the moonlight displayed.

Each whispering sigh from the trees overhead,
Carries stories of warmth where the daylight has fled.
Silvery wisps drift through the azure expanse,
Guardians of night in a shimmering dance.

I walk on the path where the quiet winds sing,
Carried away on the breath of the spring.
Yet here in this moment, I linger and dare,
To capture the frosts in the cool evening air.

With stars overhead and the moon's gentle glow,
The world feels enchanted, wrapped up in snow.
In the traces of frost, the beauty unfolds,
A tale of the night that forever beholds.

Murmurs of Ice Beneath the Stars

In the stillness of night, where shadows reside,
Murmurs of ice in the dark softly glide.
Beneath the vast heavens, the earth holds its peace,
As winter's embrace brings a moment's release.

Whispers of whispers float through the air,
A chorus of echoes that dance without care.
Frozen reflections shimmer on streams,
Carving their path through our cold, quiet dreams.

Stars twinkle bright like lanterns on high,
Guiding the wanderers who traverse the sky.
Each step on the ice brings a song to the night,
Murmurs of magic, alive in the light.

Near frozen lakes where the gentle winds sigh,
Mysteries linger while time slips on by.
In this realm of wonder, beneath starlit scars,
I find my own solace, in murmurs of stars.